AF255284

Published by Ana Carrera Hernández

A CIP record of this book is available from the British
Library.

ISBN: 978-0-9935585-5-9

Paco y los Estudiantes de Intercambio

"Paco and the Exchange Students"

Vol.2

TEACHER'S BOOK

Ana Carrera Hernández

CONTENTS

Introduction

Welcome back! As with Part 1, the aim of "*Paco y los estudiantes de intercambio, Part 2*" is to make reading in a foreign language accessible to our younger learners. To this end, Book 2 follows the structure of the textbooks most frequently used in schools in years 8 and 9 (for example, Listos 2 and Mira 2). It covers the same vocabulary and grammar so that it can be used alongside each of the units taught in the lessons, to complement the language learning and to continue developing the reading skills of the students.

Each chapter is followed by a set of accessible activity tasks. The teacher's edition also includes further suggestions on how to help students carry out these activities successfully.

The chart below, lists in brief the content and grammatical structures dealt with in each chapter of the book:

	Vocabulary	Grammatical structures
Chapter 1: "Una carta"	• Writing a letter • Describing people • Talking about activities	• Comparative • Adjectival agreement • Immediate future • Reflexive verbs • Indirect object pronouns
Chapter 2: "En el restaurante"	• Places in town • Inviting someone to go out • Making excuses • Ordering food and drink at a restaurant	• Immediate future • Sequencing words "Primero… después" • "Tengo que + infinitive"
Chapter 3: "Una pelea en el instituto"	• Saying where you went on holiday • Saying what you did on holiday • Clothes and describing what you wore	• Past tense • Opinions about past events "lo pasé bomba"
Chapter 4: "La confesión"	• Food and eating at a restaurant	• Past tense
Chapter 5: "Regreso a Inglaterra"	• Clothes • Describing what you will be wearing	• Present, past and future • *Para* + infinitive to indicate purpose • Making colours agree • Superlative (-*ísimo)*

Capítulo 1

Una carta

Theo y _________ [1] están en Inglaterra porque son las vacaciones de Navidad. Yo estoy muy triste porque me gusta Carolina pero a Theo le gusta mucho también. ¿Qué puedo hacer? Carolina es más simpática que las otras chicas del instituto y es más inteligente y divertida. Pero Theo es mi amigo y siempre es generoso y amable conmigo. ¡Qué complicado!

"—Paco, tienes una carta de Theo —dice mi madre."

Abro el sobre y leo la carta:

"¡Hola Paco! ¿Cómo estás? Aquí en Londres hace mucho frío pero no llueve. Muchas gracias por el regalo de Navidad que me envío tu madre. Me encanta la bufanda. Tu madre es muy generosa porque le mandó una bufanda para mi hermana también. Estoy muy contento porque mi primo de Colombia está aquí así que puedo practicar el español. Se llama Ricardo y tiene 12 años. Es más alto y más delgado que yo pero es mucho más feo. ¡ja, ja! Me ayuda a escribir esta carta por eso no tengo errores.

¿Qué haces ahí? Aquí normalmente me levanto muy tarde, me ducho y me visto y voy al polideportivo a jugar con mis amigos porque hace mucho frío para ir

---

[1] Write your name here.

al parque. Este fin de semana vamos a ir a casa de mi abuela en Brighton. ¡Qué bien! Me encanta Brighton porque hay playa y la gente es muy chachi. Vamos a dormir en el jardín en una tienda de campaña porque el jardín de mi abuela es gigante.

¿Cómo está Carolina? La echo mucho de menos. [2] Pienso en Carolina todos los días aunque creo que está un poco loca.

Bueno, escríbeme pronto.

Besos y abrazos

Theo"

¡Qué mal me siento! Theo es tan cariñoso. Voy a llamar a _________ [3] para pedirle consejo. De momento voy a organizar una fiesta de bienvenida para Theo y _________ [4]. Necesito pensar.

---

[2] "La echo mucho de menos": Idiomatic expression, *I miss her a lot.*
[3] Write your name here.
[4] Write your name here.

<u>Suggested activities to make full use of the text</u>

This chapter focuses on the comparative and introduces a range of adjectives to describe both physical appearance and personality. Before reading the chapter, there are several activities that could be carried out to prepare students for the grammar and the vocabulary that they will find in the story:

1. Write the adjectives below on the board. Ask students to find out the meaning by using their dictionaries, their knowledge of cognates, etc. Then, hand out mini boards (individually or in pairs). Call out one adjective and get the students to write down the person, cartoon character, animal, etc. that comes to their minds. Explain that they will need to listen carefully for the ending of the adjective, as they will be expected to write down the name of a female person if the adjective is feminine or a masculine person if the adjective is masculine. When the ending is neutral (i.e. adjectives that could be both masculine and feminine) students are allowed to choose the gender of the person:

<u>Adjectives on the board</u>

Triste	Alta
Simpatico	Delgado
Inteligente	Feo
Divertida	Loca
Generoso	Cariñoso
Amable	

2. Guess the adjective. Students work in groups of three or four. Give each group the sentences below written out on an A3 sheet of paper. Write the list of adjectives (in a random order) that they will need to fill in the gap in each sentence. The group that manages to guess where the adjectives go for each sentence wins.

a. *Carolina es más _________ que las otras chicas.*

b. *Carolina es más __________ y ____________ .*

c. *Theo es siempre ____________ y __________*

conmigo.

d. *Mi primo es más ________ y _________ que yo.*

e. *Tu madre es muy __________ porque le mandó*

una bufanda a mi hermana.

<u>Adjectives on the board</u>

Generoso	Inteligente
Simpática	Divertida
Generosa	Delgado
Alto	Amable

<u>S o l u t i o n s</u>

a. Carolina es más simpática que las otras chicas.

b. Carolina es más inteligente y divertida.

c. Theo es siempre generoso y amable conmigo.

d. Mi primo es más alto y delgado que yo.

e. Tu madre es muy generosa porque le mandó

una bufanda a mi hermana.

Alternatively, ask the students to write a letter, following the model included in this chapter, telling Paco what they are going to be doing in their Christmas holidays. To make the activity more fun, write each student's name on a small piece of paper, and get everyone to pick one piece of paper. Each student has to write a letter to the person whose name they picked, without mentioning their own name. Hand out the letters to the correct student, and get then to try and guess who wrote the letter and to explain why they think it is that person.

<u>Example</u> *"Creo que la carta la escribe Tom porque dice que va de vacaciones a Brighton y los abuelos de Tom viven en Brighton".*

Encourage students to use simple language and the present tense if they haven't learnt the past tense yet.

S t u d e n t   t a s k s :   S o l u t i o n s

1. Speaking task. Paco has called you to ask you for advice on what to do with Theo. Do you think he should tell him the truth or not? Discuss it in Spanish with your partner. Remember from previous chapters that the most important thing is to communicate your opinion. Make it simple and don't worry too much about difficult grammar. Some useful vocabulary is included below:

(No) Debería + infinitive	*He should (not) (e.g. Debería decir)*
En mi opinión	*In my opinion*
Desde mi punto de vista	*From my point of view*
Creo que	*I think that*
Estoy de acuerdo	*I agree*
No estoy de acuerdo	*I disagree*
Es una situación difícil	*It is a difficult situation*
Amistad	*Friendship*
Un amigo/una amiga	*A friend*

TIP: Before asking students to carry out this task by themselves, it is a good idea to do one model answer together with the whole class. When students struggle to communicate one point, show them how to make it simple using the present tense and the dictionary. Remind them that full sentences are not always necessary to communicate a point. Of course accuracy is important, but as long as their ideas are presented clearly, they will have successfully completed the task.

2. Reading task. Read the questions and answer them **in Spanish**. You do not need to write full sentences, just the relevant answer[5].

   a. ¿Por qué está Theo en Inglaterra?

   Porque es Navidad/ porque está de vacaciones de Navidad/ es Navidad.

   (1)

   b. ¿Cómo describe Paco a Theo?

   Generoso y amable.

   (2)

   c. ¿Qué le regaló la madre de Paco a Theo?

   Una bufanda.

   (1)

   d. ¿Adónde va a ir Theo el fin de semana?

   A casa de su abuela/ a Brighton/ a casa de su abuela en Brighton.

   (1)

   e. ¿Dónde va a dormir Theo cuando llegue a casa de la abuela?

   En el jardín/ en una tienda de campaña/ en el jardín en una tienda de campaña.

   (1)

---

[5]All the possible answers are separated by /. Any of them will be awarded a mark.

f. ¿Qué va a organizar Paco?

Una fiesta de bienvenida. (1)

3. Translation. Translate **into English** the text below. Remember that sometimes you cannot do a literal translation. After you finish translating the text, always read it over and make sure it makes sense in English. You are **not allowed** to use a dictionary.[6]

"Aquí normalmente me levanto muy tarde, me ducho y me visto y voy al polideportivo a jugar con mis amigos porque hace mucho frío para ir al parque. Este fin de semana vamos a ir a casa de mi abuela en Brighton. ¡Qué bien! Me encanta Brighton porque hay playa y la gente es muy chachi. Vamos a dormir en el jardín en una tienda de campaña porque el jardín de mi abuela es gigante".

►**Note:** Remind the students to pay particular attention to the verbs. They should underline them and determine the tense and the person. This text also has two instances of the genitive Saxon (that is, the 's construction) which does not exist in Spanish. Spend some time explaining that Spanish only has the "of" construction, so instead of saying "my grandmother's house", we should say "the house of my grandmother".

---

[6]Remember to read the whole sentence carefully as the context might help you guess the meaning of difficult words. Also, in most cases, if a Spanish word sounds like an English word, they probably mean the same!

Suggested translation:

Here, I usually get up very late, I have a shower and get dressed and I go to the sports centre to play with my friends because it is too cold to go to the park. This weekend we are going to go/we are going to my grandmother's in Brighton. Great! I love Brighton because there is a beach and the people are very cool. We are going to sleep in the garden in a tent because my grandmother's garden is huge.

Capítulo 2

En el restaurante

Es el 3 de enero y Paco, Lara y sus padres van al aeropuerto a recoger a Theo y _________ [1] que vuelven de Inglaterra. Paco está muy nervioso y Lara se burla de él[2]:

"—¿Te gusta Carolina, no? Se lo voy a decir a Theo."

"—¡Cállate! ¡Mentirosa! ¿Tú qué sabes? Eres una cotilla."

Lara se ríe y comienza a echar besos:

"—¡Muac, muac, muac! Carolina, mi amor."
"—Eres tan estúpida." Paco está muy enfadado.

Theo y _________ [3] están muy cansados pero contentos.

"—¿Cómo estás _________ [4]?—pregunta la madre de Paco."
"— ____ " [5].
"—¿Y tú, Theo?"
"—Muy bien. Inglaterra es divertida pero me gusta España mucho más porque las chicas son más bonitas..."

---

[1] Write your name here.
[2] "Se burla de él": Idiomatic expression, she makes fun of him.
[3] Write your name here.
[4] Write your name here.
[5] Tell her how you are feeling. If you are not feeling well, explain why.
E.g.: *Estoy bien pero un poco cansado porque el viaje es largo.*

Paco se pone muy nervioso. En el coche Paco le explica a Theo y __________[6] que mañana van a ir a un restaurante para darles la bienvenida.

"—¿Viene Carolina?—pregunta Theo."
"—Emm... Voy a llamarla por teléfono ahora para preguntar."

Lara mira a Paco y se ríe.

"—¡Hola, Carolina! Soy Paco... ¿Quieres salir con nosotros mañana?"
"—No sé. Tengo que hacer mis deberes y no tengo mucho dinero. ¿Qué vamos a hacer?"
"—Primero vamos a ir al restaurante a comer y después vamos a ir a la bolera. Por la noche vamos a bailar en la discoteca. Es una fiesta para dar la bienvenida a Theo y __________[7]."

Carolina recuerda lo que pasó en el cine con Theo.

"—¿Puede venir Jack? Es mi compañero de intercambio. Viene de Estados Unidos."
"—¡Claro!"—dijo Paco un poco enfadado— Quedamos a las 4.30 en la estación de autobuses."
"—¡Vale! Hasta luego."

---

[6]Write your name need.
[7]Write your name here.

Paco, Theo, Lara, __________ [8], Carolina y Jack están en el restaurante. Carolina está muy guapa. Theo no puede parar de mirarla. Paco tampoco.

"—¿Qué vais a pedir?—dice el camarero."
"—Yo quiero de primer plato una sopa de verduras y de segundo plato pollo frito con patatas, por favor—dice Paco."
"—Yo quiero una hamburguesa completa y patatas fritas. También quiero un zumo de naranja, por favor—dice Lara."
"—Yo quiero __________
____
__________ [9] ."
____

Carolina, Jack y Theo piden dos pizzas grandes con patatas fritas y nachos con queso. Theo pide una salsa muy picante.

Cuando la comida llega, Carolina y Jack comparten un nacho y se dan un beso. Paco se pone pálido y Theo casi se ahoga con su nacho picante. Lara se ríe y __________
__________ [10] .
____

---

[8] Write your name here.
[9] Write what you would like to eat and drink here.
[10] Write your name here and say what you do when you find out that Carolina and Jack are together. Use the present tense in the third person. E.g.: *Your name* abre la boca. (*your name* opens his/her mouth).

Suggested activities to make full use of the text

This chapter focuses on the use of the immediate future in the context of ordering food and arranging to go out. When reading the chapter, encourage the students to use intonation to reflect different moods and emotions.

Listed below are some suggested activities to carry out with the text in this chapter:

1. Reading for pronunciation. Hold a competition with the class. Ask one student at the front of the class to start to read the text. Every time you want another student to read (ideally the one sitting next to the first student who read), clap your hands. If a student makes a mistake with the pronunciation blow a whistle and give the class a −1 point. If any of the students can spot the problem and say the word correctly, then the class only loses half a point. If the class manages to finish the text without getting more than −8 points, they win. With the more able classes, use a timer on the board and allow them to make only 4 mistakes. After doing the activity as a whole class, students can work in pairs to continue practising the pronunciation, whilst understanding the story more clearly.

2. Reading for grammar. After having read the text for pronunciation, intonation and understanding, this chapter can be used to focus students' attention on the future tense. Ask the students to stand up, read in a louder voice, stand on their chair, clap, etc., every time they find a future tense verb. This can be done as a competition: boys against girls, one side of the class against the other or on an individual basis. If the

students make a mistake, award a point to the other team.

3. Role play. Use the dialogue in this chapter to get the students to perform small role plays in the classroom. Divide the classroom into three groups. Ask one group to prepare the role play of the journey to the airport, another to prepare the role play where Paco asks Carolina to go out, and the last group to work on the role play in the restaurant. Use props to make the role plays more realistic and fun. For example, the first group could arrange the chairs in the shape of a car, the second group could use two real telephones and the last group could use forks and plates and arrange the tables like in a restaurant. The waiter could wear a handkerchief on his/her arm. This activity can also be used as a speaking exam or in preparation for the speaking exam. Ask the students to carry out peer assessment on pronunciation, grammar, group effort, etc.

4. Guess the sentence. In this activity one student comes to the front of the class and chooses one sentence from the text to act out. The rest of the students must guess what sentence they are miming, without checking the text in the book. This exercise is good for making the students think about the vocabulary they already know and for helping them remember vocabulary by using gestures/actions.

Student tasks: Solutions

1. *Reading task.* Write a tick (√) next to the five correct sentences:

▶**Note:** Encourage students to read all the sentences and underline the key words, to save them spending too much time looking for the correct information. Focus on sentence g; students are more likely to make mistakes with this type of sentence, because they frequently skip over the presence of the negative "no", and read it as "Paco is vegetarian". This sentence is a good example of the kind of exercise that will be included in the GCSE exam, where the texts they are asked to read often do not include the exact words that appear in the questions and exercises. The text does not say if Paco is vegetarian or not, but it does say that he orders "pollo" so obviously he is not a vegetarian.

a. *Paco y su familia van al aeropuerto.* √

b. *A Theo le gusta Inglaterra más que España.*___

c. *Mañana es el cumpleaños de Theo.*___

d. *Los chicos van a ir a la discoteca.* √

e. *Jack es norteamericano.* √

f. *Van a encontrarse en la estación de tren.*___

g. *Paco no es vegetariano.* √

h. *Carolina y Jack son novios.* √

2. Speaking task. Prepare the role play below. The sentences *a to d* tell you what you will need to talk about. Think about how you will put these ideas across in Spanish:

    a. Greet the waiter.

       Buenos días.

    b. Tell him/her what you would like to eat.

       Quisiera/quiero/me gustaría (comer) ...

    c. Tell him/her what you would like to drink.

       También quisiera/quiero/me gustaría (beber) ...

    d. Tell him/her you would also like an ice cream.

       Quisiera/quiero/me gustaría un helado (de fresa, vainilla, etc.), por favor.

    e. Ask for the bill.

       La cuenta, por favor/¿Me podría traer la cuenta, por favor?

    f. Say goodbye.

       Adiós/ hasta luego.

►**Note:** This exercise helps students to familiarize themselves with the new GCSE speaking exam. You should play the part of the waiter/waitress to show students how the speaking exam will work. Alternatively, write on the board different role plays for A and B and ask students to work in pairs and practise the each role play scenario.

<table>
<tr><td valign="top" width="50%">

A

a. Greet the customer.

b. Ask him/her what he/she would like to eat.

c. Ask him/her what he/she would like to drink.

d. Ask him/her if he/she would like anything else.

e. Tell him/her you will get the bill straight away.

f. Say goodbye.

</td><td valign="top" width="50%">

B

a. Greet the waiter.

b. Tell him/her what you would like to eat.

c. Tell him/her what you would like to drink.

d. Tell him/her you would also like an ice cream.

e. Ask for the bill.

f. Say goodbye.

</td></tr>
</table>

3. *Writing task.* Design the menu for the restaurant Paco and his friends went to. Don't forget to read the text again to remind yourself what they ordered, as this must appear on the menu!

Tip: Ask students to design a menu on the computer and to decorate it. You can use this as a display in the classroom. You could also hold a competition, giving a prize to the best menu. Make sure the students make their menu for the restaurant Paco and his friends went to, to encourage them to read the information again and familiarise themselves with the relevant vocabulary.

MENÚ

Capítulo 3

Una pelea en el instituto

Paco, Theo y __________[1] se levantan muy temprano al día siguiente para ir al instituto. Theo no **pudo** dormir en toda la noche y parece un vampiro. Paco quiere contarle a Theo la verdad pero tiene miedo de que Theo se enfade mucho con él:[2]

"—
____
____ "

"—Prefiero ir andando porque estoy un poco dormido todavía —contesta Paco."

Cuando llegan al instituto ven a Carolina y a Jack. Theo quiere vomitar. Jack se acerca a saludar:

"—¡Hola! Ayer lo **pasé** bomba. **Fue** muy divertido. Gracias por invitarme."

"—¡Umm! Sí, **fue** genial—dice Theo muy poco convencido."

"—¿Estás bien? Pareces enfadado..."

"—No. Estoy muy bien. Gracias."

"—¿Sabes?[3] El año pasado **fui** a Londres. Me **gustó** mucho. **Visité** muchos museos increíbles, **saqué** un montón de fotos y **descansé** en hoteles situados cerca del Big Ben. Lo **pasé** fenomenal pero el tiempo **fue** un poco malo porque llovía todos los días. Todos los días **llevé** unos pantalones vaqueros ajustados, unos zapatos negros y un jersey de lana. También me **puse** un cinturón de cuero que **compré** en Londres."

---

[1] Write your name here.

[2] Ask whether you should walk to school or go by bus. You could use the verb "ir" conjugated in the "we" form.

[3] "¿Sabes?": This verb can be translated as "do you know what?" in order to catch the listener's attention.

"—¡Ah! Muy bien! —dijo Theo totalmente desinteresado—. Bueno, me tengo que ir. Hasta luego."

Theo se va y Jack va a hablar con Carolina:

"—Creo que Theo está enfadado conmigo. Es un poco desagradable."
"—¿Theo? Está como una cabra[4]. Un día **intentó** besarme en el cine y yo no quería."
"—¿Qué? —**dijo** Jack muy enfadado."

Jack **fue** a buscar a Theo y le gritó. Theo y Paco **empujaron** a Jack contra la pared.

A las dos de la tarde Theo y Paco **fueron** expulsados del colegio por tres días.

"—Todo esto es culpa mía —le **confesó** Lara a
.... [5] ."

Lara le **contó** todo a ....[6]:

"—
....
....
....
.... "[7]
....

---

[4]"Está como una cabra": Idiomatic expression meaning somebody is crazy. The literal translation is "to be as crazy as a goat".
[5]Write your name here.
[6]Write your name here.
[7]Write a sentence showing Lara how you feel about what she did and, if you can, offer her a possible way of sorting the situation out. You could start by saying, "Lara, creo que lo que has hecho es..." (I think what you have done is...)

Suggested activities to make full use of the text

This chapter concentrates on the use of the past tense talking about a journey to a foreign country in the context of holidays. There is also some vocabulary related to clothes.

Listed below are some suggested activities to carry out with the text in this chapter:

1. ¡Para!: This activity works better with smaller classes. Divide the students into groups of four. Give each group a piece of paper with the following passage of text (from "El año pasado fui..." to "compré en Londres") on it, but without the past verbs in bold:

"El año pasado _________ a Londres. Me _________ mucho. _________ muchos museos increíbles, _________ un montón de fotos y _______ en hoteles situados cerca del Big Ben. Lo _________ fenomenal pero el tiempo _____ un poco malo porque llovía todos los días. Todos los días _________ unos pantalones vaqueros ajustados, unos zapatos negros y un jersey de lana. También me _________ un cinturón de cuero que _________ en Londres".

Start writing a list of the missing past tense verbs (but not in the correct order) from the original text, on the interactive whiteboard. When the students think that one of the verbs on the board is the one that needs to go in the sentence, they have to stand up and shout "¡Para!" The first group that gets it right gains a point. If a group says "¡Para!" incorrectly, they lose a point. This activity will help students learn how to use the context and the words around the gaps to work out the missing words.

2. *Dictation.* Dictations are very important for students to get used to connecting spelling and pronunciation. Use the same paragraph of text from activity 1, to help the students practise writing the first person of the past tense verbs (remind them about the accent, because this is something they often forget). Read out the dictation yourself or make it into a competition between the students. Divide the students into pairs; one student dictates and the other writes down what he/she hears. They have 10 minutes to complete the exercise. At the end of the ten minutes, even if the students have not finished, put the text on the board. Get the students to correct their mistakes. Each mistake is a minus point and they must also lose a point for each word they didn't manage to write down. The pair of students with the least minus points wins. For less able classes, divide the paragraph into short sentences (see below) and give the students some time between each sentence to write down the dictation:

a. *El año pasado **fui** a Londres.*

b. ***Visité** muchos museos.*

c. ***Descansé** en hoteles modernos.*

d. *Lo **pasé** fenomenal.*

e. ***Llevé** unos pantalones vaqueros ajustados,*

f. ***Compré** un cinturón de cuero.*

3. Speaking task. Write some words from the text on the board and get the students to find ways of expressing the word in a sentence that relates to the story. This is an ideal way of getting the students to think how to communicate using the words they already know. Tell the students not to worry too much about the grammar, as long as their sentences make sense.

Example

a. *Cinturón de cuero:* "Es el cinturón que Jack compró en Londres".

b. *Vomitar:* "Theo está triste porque Jack y Carolina están juntos y quiere vomitar".

For the less able students, provide them with a speaking framework as shown below to make the exercise easier:

a. *Cinturón de cuero:* "Es el cinturón que _______________ en Londres".

b. *Vomitar:* "Theo está _________________ porque Jack y Carolina están ___________________ y quiere vomitar".

S t u d e n t   t a s k s :   S o l u t i o n s

1. Grammar task. All the verbs shown in bold in the chapter above are in the past tense. Copy them down again and write the infinitive next to them. One verb has already been done for you to show you what to do:

a. **pudo:** poder   h. **saqué:** sacar   n. **intentó:** intentar

b. **pasé:** pasar   i. **descansé:** descansar   ñ. **dijo:** decir

c. **fue:** ser   j. **pasé:** pasar   o. **fue:** ir

d. **fue:** ser   k. **fue:** ser   p. **empujaron:** empujar

e. **fui:** ir   l. **llevé:** llevar   q. **fueron:** ser

f. **gustó:** gustar   ll. **puse:** poner   r. **confesó:** confesar

g. **visité:** visitar   m. **compré:** comprar   s. **contó:** contar

►**Note:** Students are asked to write down the infinitive of the verb "fui" and "fue" several times, because sometimes the infinitive is "ir" and sometimes it is "ser". The students need to use the context to determine which is the correct infinitive to use.

2. *Translation task.* Translate **into English** the sentences below. Don't forget to read each sentence again after you have completed the exercise to make sure the translation makes sense in English:

Tip: Encourage students to find the verbs in each sentence and write down on top of the verb the tense and the person to make sure they translate them accurately. Get the students to use arrows to determine which noun the adjective is modifying. Remind students that the position of the adjective changes in English.

---

a. *Paco y Theo se levantan muy temprano al día siguiente para ir al instituto.*

Paco and Theo get up very early the next day to go to school.

b. Ayer lo pasé bomba. Fue muy divertido. Gracias por invitarme.
Yesterday I had a great time. It was really fun. Thank you for inviting me.

c. Todos los días llevé unos pantalones vaqueros ajustados, unos zapatos negros y un jersey de lana. También me puse un cinturón de cuero que compré en Londres.
Every day I wore tight jeans, black shoes and a wool jumper. Also, I put on a leather belt that I bought in London.

3. Writing task. Following Jack's description of his holiday in London, write a paragraph about your latest holiday. You **must** include:

    a. Where you went.

    b. Who you went with.

    c. What you did there.

    d. Whether you had a good time or not.

    e. The clothes you wore.

►**Note:** Remind students that they will lose marks for each point they do not include in their answer.

____

____

____

____

____

____

____
____
____
____
____
____
____
____
____
____
____
____
____
____
____
____
____
____
____
____
____
____

Tip: You can use this activity to ask students to grade somebody else's essay. Mark the grammar of the essay first (as grammar mistakes can be very difficult for young learners to spot). Then, show the students the new GCSE mark scheme for the writing (give them a simplified version). Using this mark scheme and your corrections, the students assign a mark for each section (Communication and Content, Linguistic Knowledge and Accuracy). This will help the students start to familiarise themselves with the demands of the new specifications.

Capítulo 4

La confesión

Es sábado y Paco, Theo, Lara y ______________[1] van a cenar a un restaurante. Theo está muy triste porque sus padres están furiosos. Theo siempre fue un estudiante modelo pero desde que vino a España sus notas ya no son excelentes. La madre de Paco también está muy decepcionada pero les dejó ir al restaurante porque Theo y ______________[2] van a regresar pronto para Inglaterra.

"—No te preocupes, Theo. Jack es muy arrogante y estúpido —dijo Lara para consolarle."
"—Gracias, Lara. Eres muy buena amiga."

____________[3] mira a Lara y tose.

En el restaurante los cuatro amigos pidieron de primer plato gambas y ensalada. De segundo plato pidieron una paella de marisco, excepto ______________[4] que pidió ____

____[5].

De postre todos pidieron helado de chocolate con crema y nueces. Para beber pidieron zumo de naranja y una jarra de agua.

"—Esta paella es deliciosa —dijo Paco—. El año

---

[1]Write your name here.
[2]Write your name here.
[3]Write your name here.
[4]Write your name here.
[5]Write down what you ordered here.

pasado comí una paella en este restaurante y sabía fatal. Pero ésta está muy rica."

Paco está muy nervioso y empieza a sudar. Al beber su zumo de naranja le salió por la nariz y manchó la camiseta blanca de Theo.

"—¿Estás bien? Parece que estás en la luna —dice Lara."

"—Bueno. Tengo algo que decirte. Theo. No puedo más. Antes me gustaba Carolina como a ti. Lo siento —confesó Paco."

"—Don't worry, mate —dijo Theo."

"—¿Me va a matar? —pregunta Paco pálido."

"—No, tonto. 'Mate' significa 'amigo, colega'. ¡Ja, ja, ja, ja! —aclara ___________ [6]."

"—Ya lo sabía. Era obvio. Siempre mirabas a Carolina con cara de tonto —dijo Theo—. No hay problema. Somos amigos, ¿No? Además Carolina es un poco tonta. Paso de chicas. ¿Amigos?"

"—Amigos —responde Paco."

Para celebrarlo los amigos hacen un brindis y prometen decir siempre la verdad. Lara levanta el vaso con la cara muy seria.

---

[6]Write your name here.

<u>Suggested activities to make full use of the text</u>

This chapter focuses on the use of the past tense whilst revising vocabulary related to food and drink. There is a lot of vocabulary which the students might find challenging. Remind the students that they do not need to understand every single word to be able to work with a text.

Listed below are some suggested activities to carry out with the text in this chapter:

1. Key words and cognates: Get the students to work in groups of four. Each group chooses one paragraph from the text (or, alternatively, assign one paragraph to each group). The students have five minutes to underline the words in the paragraph which help them understand what the paragraph is about[7]. Follow this up by getting them to write down what they think the key words are (in the order they come across them in the text), on a piece of paper. If they can summarise what the text is about by just looking at these key words, it shows that they have understood how to use the context and the vocabulary they know to work out the meaning of the text. Also get the students to circle the cognates. The cognates are often the key words used in the GCSE exams. Once they have completed the exercise, ask the students to feedback to the rest of the class why they chose those particular key words and to explain what the paragraph is about. This activity helps students improve their reading skills as well. Finish the exercise by showing the students how to select the

---

[7]Tell the students how many words they are allowed to select, as students usually struggle to choose single words and copy down the whole sentence.

key words, and explain that these are the words that carry the main meaning and that they are usually nouns. Students often choose words they understand (like 'también') as the key words, even though this type of word offers little insight into the content or context of the text. In the paragraph below, the key words have been underlined and then listed underneath. The cognates are written in **bold**.

Example   *Es* _sábado_ *y* _Paco, Theo, Lara_ *y* _________ *van a* _cenar_ *a un* **restaurante**. _Theo_ *está muy* _triste_ *porque sus* _padres_ *están* **_furiosos_**. _Theo_ *siempre fue un* **_estudiante modelo_** *pero desde que vino a* _España_ *sus* _notas_ *ya* _no_ *son* **excelentes**. *La* _madre de Paco_ *también está muy* **_decepcionada_** *pero les* _dejó ir_ *al* **restaurante** *porque* _Theo y_ _________ *van a* **_regresar_** *pronto para* **_Inglaterra_**.

Key words

Sábado   Paco, Theo, Lara   cenar. Theo   triste padres   furiosos   Theo estudiante modelo, España   notas   no   excelentes. Madre de Paco decepcionada   dejó   ir   restaurante   Theo y _________ regresar Inglaterra.

►**Note**: Alternatively, give the students the key words and ask them to try to guess what the paragraph is about. This will show them that very often the key words are enough to understand a text.

2. Identify the past verbs and the subject: This activity works better with able classes. Ask students to find all the past verbs in the text and determine the subject of the sentence. Note that in many cases the subject is elided so students need to rely on the verb ending to decide who the subject is. As suggested in previous chapters, this activity can be done kinaesthetically, by asking students to stand up or clap every time they see a past verb.

3. Musical: This activity requires two or three weeks of preparation on the students' part. Ask students to create their own groups (this is important as students need to feel comfortable with the people they are working with so that this activity can be successful). Students have to put together a musical using the text in this chapter. They can sing all the way through or mix representation with music. They are not allowed to change the lyrics. This activity is very creative, but also helps students understand the importance of music and rhythm to memorise vocabulary. Allow students to bring costumes and props. Ask other Spanish teachers to judge the performances or do peer assessment. Give the best group a prize as this activity requires a lot of preparation and hard work!

S t u d e n t   t a s k s :   S o l u t i o n s

1. Reading and comprehension task. Read the following sentences and complete them with a word from the box below. **There are more words than gaps!**

> **Tip:** Encourage students to pay attention to the word that goes before and after the gap. "Muy" is always followed by an adjective. Students need to decide whether the adjective is masculine or feminine, singular or plural by looking at the word it modifies. In the same way, "la" shows that the noun that follows has to be feminine and singular. Advise students to cross out the words they have already used so that they can see which words are left. It is very important to familiarise KS3 students with these basic skills.

a. *Los amigos fueron al restaurante **el fin de semana.***
b. *Los padres de Theo están muy **enfadados.***
c. *Paco cambió de opinión sobre la **paella.***
d. *Paco está muy **arrepentido** porque le mintió a su amigo.*
e. *Theo no quiere saber nada de **chicas.***
f. *Lara sabe que no está siendo **honesta** con sus amigos.*

arrepentido	enfadada	enfadados
instituto		chicas
paella		también
el fin de semana		honesta

2. Speaking task. Read the questions below and try to answer them in your own words.[8] Don't forget to justify your answers. A *yes/no* answer is not acceptable.

> **Tip:** Provide a writing framework for less able students (see the examples below). You might also want to provide students with a list of vocabulary they can use to answer these questions. However, remind students that they will not be allowed to use a dictionary in their GCSE exam, so it is a good idea for them to start getting used to using the vocabulary they already know.

a. *¿Crees que Paco es buen amigo?*

En mi opinión, creo que Paco es __________

porque ___________________________

Example *En mi opinión, creo que Paco es buen amigo porque le contó la verdad a Theo, aunque tarde.[9]*

b. *Si fueras Paco, ¿Le contarías la verdad a Theo?*

Pienso que (no) le contaría la verdad porque

____

Example *Pienso que le contaría la verdad a Theo porque es mi amigo.*

---

[8]Remember that although you should aim to be as accurate as possible, the most important thing is to be able to communicate your ideas. Always keep it simple and think about ways to state your opinion with the vocabulary you already know, wherever possible.

[9]Students will probably not be as accurate, but an answer such as "*En mi opinión, creo que Paco es buen amigo porque contar la verdad Theo, aunque tarde*", is also very good. Demand accuracy if the past tense has been covered in year 8.

c. ¿Te cae bien Lara?

Sí/ No porque Lara es ______________________

____

Example *No. porque Lara es mentirosa y no es buena amiga.*

    d. ¿ Por qué crees que Lara está seria durante el brindis?

Porque Lara ______________________________

Example *Porque Lara no le contó la verdad a Theo.*

3. Creative task. Read the chapter again and design a comic telling the story. You can use sentences taken directly from the text. You need to decide which sentences you should include in order to be able to follow the story.

►**Note:** This activity helps students summarise a long text by picking out the relevant information. Obviously, there is no one correct answer to this task; the point of the exercise is for the student to tell the story through a selection of sentences. Get the students to design their comics on a separate sheet of paper or on the computer so they can be used for display. You could award the best one a prize or print it in the school Newsletter!

Tip: For less able students, write down the sentences. The students must read and understand each sentence so that they can draw the correct images. See the example below.

PICTURE	PICTURE
Paco y sus amigos van a ir al restaurante.	En el restaurante los cuatro amigos pidieron de primer plato gambas y ensalada. De segundo plato pidieron una paella de marisco, Para beber pidieron zumo de naranja y una jarra de agua.
PICTURE	PICTURE
Paco está muy nervioso y empieza a sudar.	Tengo algo que decirte, Theo. No puedo más. Antes me gustaba Carolina como a ti. Lo siento.
PICTURE	PICTURE
No hay problema. Somos amigos, ¿No?	Para celebrarlo los amigos hacen un brindis y prometen decir siempre la verdad. Lara levanta el vaso con la cara muy seria.

Capítulo 5

El regreso a Inglaterra

Esta noche es la fiesta en el instituto para despedir a los estudiantes de intercambio. Paco y Theo fueron al centro comercial para comprar ropa nueva. Paco compró un pantalón negro, una camisa amarilla con una corbata negra con rayas azules y unos zapatos grises elegantísimos. También compró un cinturón de cuero tradicional y elegante. Theo es muy informal así que compró unos vaqueros negros de marca con una sudadera roja de manga corta y unas botas negras. También compró unas gafas de sol muy caras.

Al salir del centro comercial se encuentran a Carolina y a Jack:

"—Kill me now — dice Theo."

"—¡Hola! ¿Habéis comprado muchas cosas? Yo voy a ir guapísima. Para ir a la fiesta voy a llevar un vestido rojo largo con lentejuelas y unos zapatos de tacón preciosos. Voy a ser la chica más elegante de la fiesta. ¿Verdad, Jack? —dice Carolina."

Theo mira para Paco y le dice:

"—Hey! No voy a la fiesta. No soporto a esta niña."

"—Yo tampoco. ¿Nos vamos al cine?"

"—¡Siiiiiiiiii! —dice Theo desesperadamente."

Paco y Theo dejan la ropa nueva en casa, se ponen un chándal y van a ver una película de acción. Cuando entran en la sala hay una niña sentada sola mirando fijamente la pantalla.

"—¡Lara! ¿Qué haces aquí? —pregunta Paco."

"—Tenía ganas de estar sola."

"—¿Qué te pasa? —pregunta Theo."

"—Theo, soy una amiga muy mala. Yo fui la que te puso la mano encima en el cine cuando estabas con Carolina. Era una broma pero todo se complicó."

"—¿Qué? ¡Lara! Eres... —Theo se detuvo y respiró hondo— Bueno, es igual. Al final me hiciste un favor porque Carolina es tonta. No me gusta nada."

En el aeropuerto, Paco y Lara están muy tristes porque van a echar mucho de menos a Theo y a _______[1].

"—¿Lo pasasteis bien en España? —pregunta la madre de Paco."

"—Sí, lo pasé de maravilla. Muchas gracias por todo dice Theo."

---

[1]Write your name here.

"—¿Y tú, _______?"[2]

"—
____

____ "[3] .

Es el 31 de agosto. Han pasado ocho años desde que Theo y _______ [4] se fueron de la casa de Lara y Paco. Ahora es Lara la que está en el aeropuerto preparándose para ir de intercambio a Londres. Su familia adoptiva la está esperando en el aeropuerto. Lara está muy nerviosa porque su inglés no es muy bueno. Cuando recoge su equipaje y sale a buscar a su familia se quedó pálida:

"—Theo?"

---

[2]Write your name here.
[3]Tell Paco´s mum whether you had a good time or not.
[4]Write your name here.

Suggested activities to make full use of the text

The last chapter of the book includes present, past and future verbs and focuses mainly on the vocabulary related to clothes. Carry out the activities listed below before reading the chapter to help prepare the students for the new vocabulary they will come across in the text:

1. Catwalk. Divide the students into groups of four or five. Tell them that the characters in the book (Paco, Theo, Carolina, Jack and Lara) are going to a party. Each group must decide what the different characters are going to wear. Bring some clothes to the lesson so that the students can dress up. One student in each group describes the clothes, while another student catwalks in the clothes. You can even play music in the background to make it more realistic. Alternatively, assign each group only one character to make the activity easier (especially for lower ability students). To prepare the students for the vocabulary in this chapter, encourage them to describe the material of the clothes.

Example   *Una camisa de algodón amarilla* instead of *una camisa.*

2. Guess who. Provide students with a variety of clothes (see below). They need to decide who is wearing them and explain why.

Example *Creo que Paco lleva un pantalón negro porque Paco es formal.*

Give students 10 minutes to make their decisions and justifications. The students who manage to guess the most answers correctly get a prize. This game can also be played in pairs or groups.

¿Paco, Theo o Carolina?

1. *Lleva una camisa amarilla.* **Paco**

2. *Lleva unos vaqueros negros de marca.* **Theo**

3. *Lleva unos zapatos de tacón preciosos.* **Carolina**

4. *Lleva una corbata negra con rayas azules.* **Paco**

5. *Lleva un vestido rojo con lentejuelas.* **Carolina**

6. *Lleva unos zapatos grises.* **Paco**

7. *Lleva una sudadera roja de manga corta.* **Theo**

8. *Lleva unas botas negras.* **Theo**

9. *Lleva unas gafas de sol muy caras.* **Theo**

10. *Lleva un cinturón de cuero tradicional.* **Paco**

3. Discussion. This is the last chapter of the book, so the students will be curious about how the story is going to end. Ask the students some questions about the chapter before reading it, so they can try and guess what happens. This will encourage them to read the text so that they can find out what actually happens. They can give themselves a point for each thing they guessed correctly. This activity can be done as a class orally or as a quiet, individual written

task. Remind students that yes/no answers are not allowed. Here are some suggestions for the type of questions to ask:[5]

a. ¿Qué crees que va a hacer el colegio de Paco para despedir a los estudiantes de intercambio?

(What do you think Paco's school is going to do to say farewell to the exchange students?)

b. ¿Crees que Paco y Theo se van a reconciliar con Carolina?

(Do you think Paco and Theo will finally get on with Carolina?)

c. ¿Crees que Lara le va a contar la verdad a Theo?

(Do you think Lara is going to tell Theo the truth?)

d. Lara va a ir de viaje cuando sea mayor, ¿Sabes adónde?

(Lara is going to travel when she is older, do you know where?)

---

[5]Lower ability classes might find this task too challenging if they have to write the answer in Spanish. Give them three options and ask them to choose one. Able students should be encouraged to produce their own answers. Remind them not to overcomplicate their answers and to conjugate the verbs properly. Allow them to use the dictionary for new vocabulary.

Student tasks: Solutions

1. Vocabulary task. Use the mannequins below to draw the clothes that Paco, Theo and Carolina bought to go to the party.

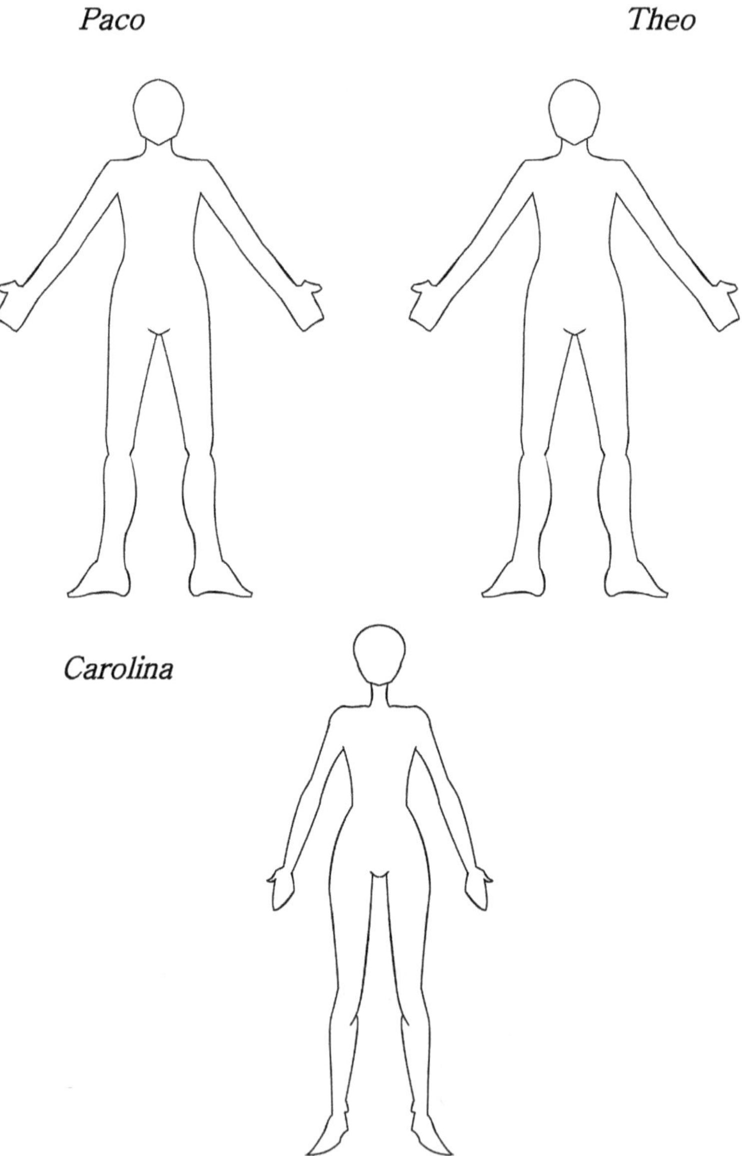

Paco: Un pantalón negro, una camisa amarilla con una corbata negra con rayas azules y unos zapatos grises muy elegantes. También compró un cinturón de cuero tradicional y elegante.

(Black trousers, a yellow shirt with a blue stripped tie and very elegant black shoes. Also, a traditional, elegant leather belt.)

Theo: Unos vaqueros negros de marca con una sudadera roja de manga corta y unas botas negras. También compró unas gafas de sol muy caras.

(Black designer jeans with a red, short-sleeved sweatshirt and black boots. Also, very expensive sunglasses.)

Carolina: Un vestido rojo largo con lentejuelas y unos zapatos de tacón preciosos.

(A long dress with sequins and high-heeled shoes.)

2. Writing task. Imagine you have been invited to the school party. Describe the clothes you are going to wear using the future tense. You must include:

a. The colour and the pattern of the different items you are wearing (de cuadros, de lunares, de manga corta, de cuero, etc.).

b. The type of shoes you are wearing.

c. Your opinion about the different items you are wearing (E.g.: Voy a llevar una blusa blanca muy elegante).

You can use the sentence below to start your description:

Para ir a la fiesta voy a llevar ...

Tip: Remind students that they must include all the points above. Provide students with a model to follow. This activity is useful for putting new vocabulary into practice. Ask the students to translate the model into English first and then correct it in the classroom, so that they can use it to form their own ideas for their descriptions.

Here are two paragraphs that can be used to model the activity both to able and less able students:

Able students

Chico: Para ir a la fiesta voy a llevar ropa muy elegante. Primero llevaré unos pantalones negros de seda con un cinturón de cuero de color dorado. También llevaré una camisa de manga larga de cuadros azules y blancos pero no llevaré corbata porque es incómoda. Prefiero llevar una pajarita de color blanco con lunares negros. Igualmente, voy a llevar unos zapatos grises con un poco de tacón. Si hace frío, llevaré una chaqueta de lana o una americana a juego con los pantalones y la camisa. La ropa será muy cómoda pero tradicional y formal. Me gusta ir formal porque parezco mayor.

Chica: Para ir a la fiesta voy a llevar un vestido corto rojo de lunares negros con un lazo blanco en la espalda. El vestido es de algodón pero llevaré una torera de seda muy elegante. Si hace frío, voy a llevar medias transparentes y unos zapatos de tacón de terciopelo negros o marrones. Prefiero el terciopelo que el charol porque en mi opinión es más elegante. También voy a llevar un bolso negro con lentejuelas y un collar de perlas blancas. En el pelo voy a llevar un moño pequeño con una diadema de brillantes.

Less able students

Chico: Para ir a la fiesta voy a llevar ropa muy elegante. Primero llevaré unos pantalones negros de seda con un cinturón de cuero. También llevaré una camisa de manga larga y cuadros pero no llevaré corbata porque es incómoda. Prefiero una pajarita blanca con lunares negros. Voy a llevar unos zapatos grises. Si hace frío, llevaré una americana azul o negra. La ropa será muy cómoda pero tradicional y formal.

Chica: Para ir a la fiesta voy a llevar un vestido corto rojo de lunares. También llevaré una torera de seda muy elegante. Si hace frío, voy a llevar medias y unos zapatos de tacón de terciopelo negros o marrones. Además voy a llevar un bolso negro con lentejuelas y un collar de perlas blancas.

3. Translation task. Find the translation in Spanish in the text, for the phrases/sentences below:

    a. I can't stand this girl.

No soporto a esta niña.

    b. I am going to be the most elegant girl in the party.

Voy a ser la chica más elegante de la fiesta.

    c. Me neither.

Yo tampoco.

    d. I don't like her at all.

No me gusta nada.

    e. Did you have a good time?

¿Lo pasasteis bien en España?

4. Speaking task. Prepare a one minute presentation explaining how you would continue the story. As always, remember to keep it simple and use the vocabulary you already know (although you may use a dictionary, if necessary). Don't forget to conjugate the verbs paying attention to whether they should be in the present, past or future. You can use the space below to make notes.

►**Note:** This activity can be used for a speaking assessment. Give students a week or two to prepare it. Allow students to make a PowerPoint presentation to aid them with their speech, using pictures and single words. They can even create a short story about what is going to happen and present it to the rest of the class. Less able students will need a framework to follow; provide them with a variety of options they can choose from. This framework can also be given to the very able students to provide them with ideas. See the example below:[6]

*"Creo que Lara **a.**_________________________.*
*Después Lara **b.**_________________________.*
*Paco **c.**_________________________. Por otro*
*lado Carolina **d.**_________________________. Al final*
*Lara **e.**_________________________ ".*

a.   1. Se va a enamorar de Theo.

        2. Se va a querer cambiar de familia.

        3. Regresará a España con su familia.

        4. ...

b.   1. Va a quedarse a vivir en Londres para siempre.

        2. Va a enamorarse de otro chico y Theo se va a deprimir.

        3. Se arrepentirá y le escribirá una carta a Theo.

        4. ...

---

[6] I have included both the immediate future (voy a+ infinitive) and the simple future (comparé, iré, etc.). If only one of these future tenses has been taught, please adjust the activity so that students can access it more easily.

c. 1. Viajará a Londres a visitar a su amigo Paco y se enamorará de su prima.

2. Viajará a Londres para convencer a su hermana que Paco es un amigo.

3. Irá de intercambio unos meses a visitar a su amigo.

4. ...

d. 1. Se enamorará de Paco y le pedirá perdón.

2. Le escribirá una cara a Theo para perdirle perdón.

3. Se casará con Jack y se irá a Estados Unidos.

4. ...

e. 1. Se casará con Theo.

2. Echará de menos España y dejará a Theo.

3. Se casará con Jack.

4. ...